Jacob

by James Poole

ISBN: 978-1-78364-458-2

The Open Bible Trust
Fordland Mount, Upper Basildon,
Reading, RG8 8LU, UK.

www.obt.org.uk

Jacob

Contents

Introduction

Of all the four patriarchs, God's choice of Jacob is a mystery to many. Abraham's great faith (Hebrews 11:17-19) earned him the title of "the father of all who believe" (Romans 4:11). Timid and sensitive Isaac learned the great lesson that "the fear of man brings a snare but whoso puts his trust in Jehovah shall be safe" (Proverbs 29:25). Joseph stands out in a class by himself – a perfect type of Christ in His humiliation and exaltation.

But what have we to learn from Jacob? He was a heel and a supplanter, a man of low morals, scheming and plotting his own will, trying to bring about God's blessing in his way! But as we look upon the life of Jacob, do we not behold a wondrous God of love and grace, Who patiently dealt with unworthy Jacob, disciplining him, guiding him, and at last bringing him to that place where he learned that God alone rules. And so Jacob's name was changed to Israel, meaning "God commands or orders" (Genesis 32:24-28).

Such a story of glorious grace and unchanging love, written for our learning, is surely a comfort to us, for the God of Jacob is our God too!

Jacob: Contrasts

The first period of Jacob's life is contained in Genesis chapters 28-34. In it we see the *restlessness* of unbelief portrayed. In the second period 46-49, we see the *restfulness* of faith.

To Abraham God said,

> "I will make of thee a great nation and I will bless thee and make thy name great and thou shalt be a blessing" (Genesis 12:2).

To Isaac was added the promise of God's protection and presence (Genesis 26:3). To Jacob, beside the protection and presence of God, were added promises of preservation and restoration (Genesis 28:15).

The complete fulfilment of these promises awaits the time of Israel's restoration. In that future age of physical and spiritual blessing, the nation of Israel, under the rule of the Lord Jesus Christ, as their Messiah, will be a preserved and restored nation. A marvel and a blessing to all nations.

It is a cause for wonder, adoration, and praise of God's infinite grace that to Jacob, who by human standards is the least worthy of the four patriarchs, should be given the highest revelation of God's promises to Israel.

Our blessings in Christ Jesus are far different from those promised to Israel. Our spiritual blessings are not on earth, but in the heavenly realms, but they are ours because of the exceeding riches of His grace (Ephesians 1:3; 2:7). What humility of mind it calls for in us to walk worthy of such a high calling (Ephesians 4:1).

Jacob's birth

Jacob was the twin brother of Esau and when Rebecca was pregnant, the children struggled together in her womb. She enquired of the Lord as to why this was so. The answer God gave was that the children represented two peoples, one stronger than the other, and that the older shall serve the younger (Genesis 25:23 RAV).

When the children were born Esau came out first, followed by Jacob, whose hand took hold of Esau's heel. So he was named Jacob, which means "supplanter" (Genesis 25:25-26 RAV).

God's choice of Jacob

God's choice was made before the twins were born.

> "Not having done any good or evil that the purpose of God regarding election might stand, not of works but of Him Who calls" (Romans 9:11 RAV).

> "Jacob I have loved but Esau I have hated" (v 13).

This was a quotation from Malachi 1:2-4, which shows how the prophecy to Rebecca was fulfilled and also explains how God manifests His love and His hatred.

That the conduct of Esau and Jacob after their birth, and the subsequent characters of the two peoples, did not influence God's choice, is stated in verse 11 above. There are such emotions as love and hatred in God, but we must not import into the Divine hatred, the malice and vindictiveness which makes human hatred so wicked. God's hatred is holy. His righteousness cannot but hate sin. There is no such thing as an undeserved hatred in God. God is good to the hateful as He is good to all and His tender mercies are over all his works. Esau, though a profane man, was blessed with earthly blessings.

God's love to Jacob was, as history shows, a gracious and unmerited love which persisted in spite of many provocations. Jacob was taught to regard Esau, the Edomite, with natural affection. God had said,

> "Thou shalt not abhor an Edomite, for he is thy brother" (Deuteronomy 23:7).

The sovereignty of God

God is sovereign. He has the unfettered right to choose whom He will for blessing. Similarly He hardens whom He will (Romans 9:18). But before we jump to a hasty conclusion that we are subject to blind fate and we are merely "puppets on strings", let us consult the case of the hardening of Pharaoh's heart.

God hardened Pharaoh's heart in order to display His power in the deliverance of Israel from Egypt. I have looked up all the references to the hardening of Pharaoh's heart in the book of Exodus. Let us consider them in chronological order.

The first seven references do not mention the Lord as doing the hardening, but rather Pharaoh himself, with the apparent exception of chapter 7:13. However, there the rendering should be, according to the Hebrew, "and Pharaoh's heart was hardened". There is no mention of the Lord in this verse.

The subsequent references all state that the Lord hardened Pharaoh's heart, in order to display His Divine power. God's sovereignty and human accountability thus go hand in hand. Israel in the Old Testament were often exhorted not to harden their hearts (Psalm 95:8).

It was only after God's infinite patience gave out, at the end of Acts[1], that Paul pronounced the final sentence of blindness and deafness brought on by that nation's hardened heart. By the Holy Spirit he quoted Isaiah 6:9-10, and for a season Israel has become *lo ammi*, not my people (see Acts 28:25-28).

There is a solemn lesson for us all who are privileged to hear God's gospel concerning His Son today. It is sad that one may become "gospel hardened", having heard it many times and not

---

[1] For more on this see *The Beginning and End of the Acts of the Apostles* by Michael Penny, published by The Open Bible Trust.

responded to it. The same sun that melts the wax hardens the clay.

Jacob's deceitful act

We are all familiar with the despicable trick Jacob played on Esau and later Isaac, to obtain the blessing of the birthright by deceit. This later deceit was organised by Rebecca who, in spite of the fact that the Lord had informed her at the birth of the twins that Esau, the elder, should serve Jacob, the younger, attempted to bring this about by her own device (Genesis 27).

Yet, when Isaac realised that Jacob had deceived him by disguising himself as his brother Esau, he saw the hand of God in this and having blessed Jacob with the birthright, would not change his mind, although Esau sought his father's favour with tears (Genesis 27:38; Hebrews 11:20).

Nevertheless Isaac blessed Esau with earthly blessings, as a profane man, without imparting the spiritual privileges of the first born son (Genesis 27:39-40).

Jacob's flight from Esau

Esau hated Jacob, who had stolen the birthright from him, and sought to slay him. This reached the ear of Rebecca who persuaded Jacob to flee to her brother Laban, at Haran. So Jacob became a fugitive and was destined never to see the face of his mother again. As he slept on the ground, in an open field at Luz with his head pillowed on a stone, a fugitive from his home and his own country, the Lord was revealed to him in a dream (Jacob's ladder – Genesis 28:12-15 NIV). Here, in this first appearance of God to Jacob, unconditional promises were made to him.

On awakening out of his sleep, Jacob made a vow that if God would keep His word to him, then he would acknowledge the Lord as his God (Genesis 28:20-22). Note Jacob's attitude. If God would keep His word! Jacob did not wholly trust the Lord.

Jacob journeys to Laban his uncle

Jacob's immediate concern was for "bread to eat and raiment to put on". Yet instead of leaning wholly upon God's promises to him to supply these needs, he takes things into his own hands and seeks, by cunning and natural ability, to provide these things for himself in the employment of his uncle Laban, in an alien land, thus laying the foundation of twenty whole years of frustration and vexation. But each act of insubordination of a believer sets in motion checks that will eventually curb it.

Jacob's restless anxiety for material things, combined with his cunning and natural ability, if successful, might have left Jacob satisfied in an alien land. So God uses the trickery and meanness of Laban to check this inclination in Jacob and keep alive his longing for the Land of Promise.

Laban's craftiness

Now Laban, Jacob's uncle, was a mean, crafty, and unscrupulous man. He sought to get out of Jacob all he could for his personal advantage, giving as little as he needed in return for Jacob's services.

At the very first, when Jacob fell in love with Rachel his daughter and agreed with Laban to serve him for seven years for her, he was cheated of her by Laban's substitution of Leah (Genesis 29:22-25).

The result of this was that Laban forced Jacob to serve him for another seven years to obtain Rachel as his wife. During the fourteen years in servitude to Laban, the fathers of eleven of the tribes of Israel were born (Genesis 29:32-30:24). Benjamin the father of the twelfth tribe was born later (Genesis 35:18).

The time at last came when Jacob decided to leave the service of Laban and return to his own country.

Laban, cautions as ever and realising that the presence of Jacob meant prosperity for himself, tried to make him stay. But Jacob had had enough of Laban and so they discussed wages for a final settlement.

Jacob's cunning scheme

Now due to Jacob's care and the Lord's blessing, Laban's cattle had increased enormously from small beginnings. Instead of asking for money Jacob hit upon a plan to enrich himself, at Laban's expense, by requesting livestock (Genesis 30:31-33). Laban, thinking that he would outwit, Jacob, removed all the best cattle and gave them to his sons to hide three days journey away (Genesis 30:35-36).

But Jacob, with the cattle that remained, used his knowledge of their breeding habits and the physical and psychological effect of their surroundings. Jacob devised a scheme to make sure of obtaining his wages from Laban. (Genesis 30:37-43 NIV). Thus Jacob prospered himself enormously at Laban's expense.

But before Jacob had put his scheme into effect, the Lord had said to him in a dream,

"Look up and see that all the male goats mating with the flock are streaked, speckled or spotted, for I have seen all that Laban has been doing to you" (Genesis 31:12 NIV).

So Jacob devised a scheme to gain possession of the choicest livestock, in spite of the fact that the Lord had told him before he put his plan into operation that He would give him the flocks! This act of Jacob, to try and help out God, though it gained for him much livestock, made the Lord's promise appear to be based on a fraud.

Neither Laban nor his sons knew of the vision Jacob had received from the Lord. All they could see was summed up in the words of Laban's sons,

"Jacob has taken away all that was our father's; and of that which was our father's hath he gotten all this glory" (Genesis 31:1).

Jacob's flight from Laban

Having got himself into all this mess, Jacob tries to get out of it by his own methods. It is a fact that one false step leads to another. Jacob now, fearing greatly and not knowing what action he might take, decides to leave his uncle secretly. Laban pursued his nephew and overtook him at Mizpah, where a heated argument took place between the two men.

What a sad and sorry figure Jacob cuts at Mizpah! His wives were acquired by slavery in his uncle's service. His children were Laban's by law. His vast hoards of livestock were acquired by deception and now only God's intervention on his behalf, saved him out of the hand of Laban.

Though God was with Jacob at Padan-aram, during his sojourn there, He was not with Jacob in his acts! There was nothing in Jacob's behaviour to mark him, in the eyes of men, as being God's chosen one. Laban would probably never have known this but for God's direct communication to him, restraining him from harming him (Genesis 31:24).

Had Jacob listened to the angel of the Lord in his vision, he would still have gained the livestock without resorting to trickery, but, more than that, the Lord would have received recognition from Laban that He was the protector of His servant Jacob. As it was, Jacob acquired the livestock with sorrow and missed the great blessing – the privilege of being God's witness to men! Laban reforms, and he and Jacob make a covenant together that they will, henceforth, do no harm to each other (Genesis 31:44-53).

This lesson is written for our blessing also. It is the story of a man who did not trust in the Lord with all his heart, of a man who did lean on his own understanding. Note the consequences of disobedience – restlessness and unprofitability in God's service.

Jacob meets Esau his brother

Jacob now journeys on and the Lord opens his eyes to behold the unseen heavenly hosts which camped round him to protect him (Genesis 32:1-2). Surely such a vision should cast out all fear from Jacob, but no! Great fear grips him as he journeys towards the land of Seir, the country of Edom, where dwells his brother Esau. Would Esau seek vengeance upon his brother?

Jacob sends messengers before him to Esau, to prepare the ground for reconciliation between them (Genesis 32:3-5). But the messengers return with the alarming news that Esau was on his way to meet Jacob with four hundred armed men. Now is the test of faith! In spite of the heavenly vision of unseen heavenly hosts to protect him, Jacob resorts to his own plan.

He divides his people into two camps, hoping that if Esau attacked, one company of his people would be able to flee and be saved. Having done this Jacob resorts to prayer to the Lord for deliverance, ignoring the promise of protection the Lord had given him in the heavenly vision! But he finds no peace of mind and plans further. He must give his brother Esau a massive present of various kinds of livestock, hoping that when he and Esau meet, face to face, he would be appeased and accept him.

For their safety, Jacob took his two wives and eleven sons and passed over the ford Jabbok (which means "pouring out or emptying"), for Jacob was now left alone. He had sent over all that he had!

Jacob at Peniel comes face to face with God

But now the Lord sets Himself to conquer Jacob's independence. That night there wrestled a man, the Angel of the Lord, with Jacob. Such a strong resistance of Jacob had to be broken, so the Lord puts Jacob's thigh out of joint. This crippled him for the rest of his life (Hebrews 11:21), and is symbolic of his need to depend upon the Lord.

"Let me go," said the Wrestler. "I will not let thee go except Thou bless me", replied Jacob, still persisting in the struggle. But how could the Lord bless self-willed and insubordinate Jacob?

"What is thy name?" said the Wrestler. "Jacob" (the supplanter) was the answer.

> "Thy name shall no more be called Jacob but Israel (God rules), for thou hast striven with God and man and hast prevailed".

This may seem a paradox, but prevailing prayer gives one a greater awareness of God's sovereignty.

Jacob had contended for the birthright and succeeded. He had contended for the blessing and had succeeded. He had contended with Laban and succeeded. Now he contends with God and prevails. Hence his name was changed to Israel – God rules, to teach him the greatly needed lesson for dependence upon God (Genesis 32:24-28).

What a lesson for us! Let us trust in the Lord with all our heart and lean not on our own understanding. In all our ways acknowledge Him and He shall direct (rightly divide) our paths (Proverbs 3:5-6). In all our trials and testings, may our trust in God be steadfast!

And what of the meeting with brother Esau? Jacob's worst fears were not realised. Esau was genuinely glad to see his brother. He ignored the elaborate procession and ceremony delivered by Jacob. He did not want to accept the gift, but Jacob insisted.

Jacob's faith obedience

God, all along, had been Jacob's Protector, just as He had promised. This was in spite of Jacob's unbelief. In acknowledgment of this Jacob built an altar, calling it *El Elohe Israel*, which means "God, the God of Israel" (Genesis 33:20). This he did on meeting Esau and coming to Shalem, a city of Schechem in the land of Canaan, where he pitched his tent before the city.

This action put Jacob in danger of compromising with the idolatrous people and environment about him. This was not the right place to stay, so the Lord intervened and said to Jacob,

> "Arise, go up to Bethel and dwell there and make there an altar unto God that appeared unto thee when thou didst flee from thy brother Esau" (Genesis 35:1).

Jacob then purified himself and his household and put away their strange gods (an indication of how far they had compromised with the inhabitants and customs of the land of Canaan). Then the fear of God was upon the cities that were round about and they did not attack Jacob and his household. God was his Protector!

Thus Jacob learned the dangers of a blind faith at the expense of truth and the blessedness of the effectual working of a living trust in God. It is incumbent upon Pastors, Evangelists and Teachers of God's word, "to declare the whole counsel of God" and not just bits of it. There is also the temptation "to sugar the pill" and so take the cutting edge off God's Word.

Jacob's return to Bethel

What were Jacob's feelings on his return to Bethel – to the very place from where he had set out upon his journey? God had promised to bring him again into this land and here was the very fulfilment of His promise. In spite of his waywardness, God had kept him in all faithfulness wherever he went. What an anchorage for his faith when God's promise of restoration was realised.

One of my favourite hymns is *Great is Thy faithfulness*. When I look back over my life, I can see how faithful God has been to me! I can, in a sense say, my name is no longer Jacob but Israel, "God rules!"

Jacob's faith tested

Jacob's faith was soon put to the test. Death enters Jacob's household. This was a sad blow to Jacob, who doubtless found in the nurse Deborah some consolation and reminder of his mother Rebecca, whom he had not seen for years and was destined never to see again in this life. In the midst of Jacob's sorrow over Deborah, God again appears to him to comfort him and bless him, by turning his mind away from his sorrow to the great and mighty promises He had made.

> "God said to him, 'Your name is Jacob but you will no longer be called Jacob, your name will be Israel'. So He called his name Israel and God said to him, 'I am God almighty; be fruitful and increase in number. A nation and a community of nations will come from you, and kings will come from your body. The land I gave to Abraham and Isaac, I also give to you, and I will give this land to your descendants after you'" (Genesis 35:10-12 NIV).

Two great sorrows now follow, the death of his beloved wife Rachel and his son Reuben having sexual intercourse with Bilhah, Jacob's concubine.

But Jacob's faith in God shines through it all! When the dying mother Rachel named her new born babe *Benoni*, son of my sorrows, Jacob changed it to *Benjamin*, son of my right hand!

Thus Jacob turns his mind from contemplating things, as they existed round about him, to the future promises of God. He sees the working out of the Divine plan amidst the misery of his present sorrows. His faith in God remains firm.

Jacob meets Joseph

Many years now elapse, during which the history of Joseph, Jacob's cherished son, predominates. We will take up the threads of Jacob's life again, where he sets out from Hebron for the land of Egypt, to meet his son Joseph.

The Jacob of old would not have consented to go down to Egypt, but Israel sought the Lord for guidance. Must he go down to Egypt? Was it not there that Abraham had faltered in his faith? Was not Isaac warned not to go there? Preoccupied with such thoughts, Jacob came to Beersheba.

What memories cluster round this place! There, Abraham met the supreme test of his faith, the offering of Isaac as a sacrifice. There God appeared to Isaac and King Abimelech came to acknowledge him as the blessed one of Jehovah. From there, too, Jacob began his wanderings. Here Jacob called upon God for guidance, offering sacrifices. God's answer was "I will go down to Egypt with thee" (Genesis 46:3-4).

So Jacob went down to Egypt, surrounded by the divine presence. The meeting of Jacob and Joseph his son at Goshen, on the way to Egypt, is one of the most emotional events of the Bible! After all the sorrowful years of believing that Joseph, the apple of his eye, was dead ... Oh the joy when they met!

> "As soon as Joseph appeared before him, he threw his arms around his father and wept for a long time" (Genesis 46:29 NIV).

Jacob blesses Joseph's sons

Jacob's faith and spiritual perception now shone supremely. Contrary to Joseph, who expected Manasseh his first born son to receive the blessing of the birthright.

Israel by faith blessed Ephraim (Genesis 48:14-19). In the blessing of Jacob's own sons, upon his death bed, he interprets the history of them as the consummation of the nation of Israel's history. So ends the life of one of the most undeserving men – Jacob, yet he was a foil to the super-abounding grace of God!

Lessons from the life of Jacob

In the whole life of Jacob, two outstanding lessons emerge;

1) grace overcoming the will of the flesh, and
2) faith overcoming the fear of man.

The first part of Jacob's life shows us the disastrous effects of trying to obtain a good result by self-effort and unholy means. This subtle temptation meets us at every turn, not only as individuals but collectively. How often has the church sought the support of earthly sovereignty and blessing instead of holding fast to our heavenly calling and destiny in the heavenly realms? We are blessed with every spiritual blessing[2] in Christ there (Ephesians 1:3).

---

[2] For more on this see *Spiritual Blessing in Heavenly Realms* by Brian Sherring, published by The Open Bible Trust.

"Minding earthly things", is not to be confused with our daily duties, in home or at work, and the moderate use of healthy recreation. It is when those things take the priority in our lives that service for the Lord takes second place.

Another, more subtle form of "minding earthly things" is the attempt to pillage the things that exclusively belong to Israel, their Divine calling, which is to bring spiritual and material blessing to this earth, when they repent and acknowledge Christ as their Messiah. Let us be content with the heavenly calling above in the heavenly realms in Christ Jesus.

Having said all this, I do not want to give the impression that Christians should ignore and be callous about the plight today of suffering humanity. One cannot help being deeply moved by what one reads in the newspapers and sees on television, about conditions abroad and in our own country. It is only right that we should give some help to these needy people, by prayer and supplication, by the giving of money and support to those organisations that attempt to alleviate those in need.

But, and this is important, we must not be so absorbed in humanitarian work that we neglect our primary role of proclaiming the Gospel, which Paul preaches in his epistle to the Romans, and building up the saints in that calling above in Christ Jesus, expounded in Ephesians, Philippians and Colossians.

Satan will do all he can to stop us from fruitful preaching and teaching of the word of God during this dispensation of God's grace. This he does by concentrating our efforts on welfare and neglecting our vital priority of teaching spiritual things. It is good and merciful to give bread to the starving. It is even better to include with it Christ, the Bread of life! Let us hold fast to our faith without wavering and our calling above in Christ Jesus. Let us not be tossed about by every wind and wave of doctrine, but grow up in all things into Him our Head, Christ Jesus.

More on Jacob

Portraits of the Patriarchs

By William Henry, Andrew Marple, Michael Penny and Sylvia Penny

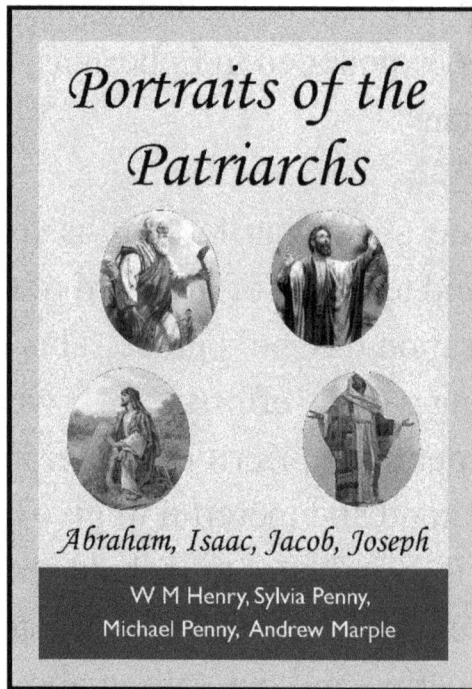

Portraits of the Patriarchs is based on Abraham, Isaac, Jacob and Joseph.

The four authors do an excellent job of not only bringing before us the important issues in the lives of the four patriarchs (i.e. lessons in history). However, they also, in considering the lives and experiences of Abraham, Isaac, Jacob and Joseph, draw out lessons of faith and practice which are applicable to 21st century Christians.

****

Further details of this book can be seen on
www.obt.org.uk

It can be ordered from the website
and also from

The Open Bible Trust,
Fordland Mount, Upper Basildon,
Reading, RG8 8LU, UK.

It also available as an eBook
from Amazon and Apple,
and also as a KDP paperback from Amazon.

Free sample

For a free sample of
the Open Bible Trust's magazine *Search*,
please email

admin@obt.org.uk

or visit

www.obt.org.uk/search

About the author

James Poole was born in Finchley, London, in 1909 and took a course in Business Training at the City of London College. During his working years he was employed by various institutions and banks in the City of London. When he wrote this booklet he was enjoying retirement with his wife in Eastbourne, Sussex, but has since fallen asleep in Christ.

Also by James Poole

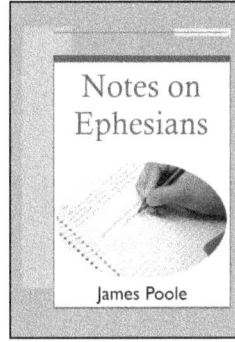

Further details of all the books here can be seen
on **www.obt.org.uk**

The can be ordered from the website
and also from

The Open Bible Trust,
Fordland Mount, Upper Basildon,
Reading, RG8 8LU, UK.

They are also available as eBooks
from Amazon and Apple,
and also as KDP paperbacks from Amazon.

Further Reading

Approaching the Bible
Michael Penny

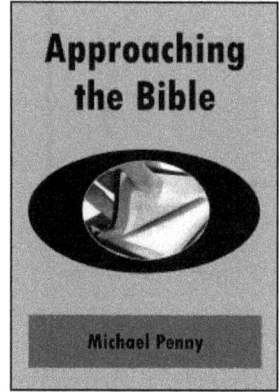

In easy to understand steps, and with many interesting examples, Michael Penny provides the rational for the view that before we try to *apply* any passage in the Bible to ourselves, we should discover first what it meant to those to whom its words were initially addressed. The book advocates that this is best done by considering the passage under the following headings:

1) **W**ho said or wrote it;
2) to **W**hom was it said or written, or concerning **W**hom was it said or written;
3) **W**here it was said or written, or concerning **W**here was it said or written;
4) **W**hat was said or written;
5) **W**hen was it said or written, or concerning **W**hen was it said or written;
6) **W**hy was it said or written.

Applying these six **"W"** rules puts the passage into its proper context and gives us the right perspective on it. Only after doing this can we determine:

7) **W**hether the passage applies to our situation and what the correct application is.

It is the *consistent* use of these **Seven Ws** which helps us discover the right and relevant application of any passage to our lives.

****

This book, and the one on the next page, can be ordered from **www.obt.org.uk** and from

The Open Bible Trust,
Fordland Mount, Upper Basildon,
Reading, RG8 8LU, UK.

40 Problem Passages
Michael Penny

This book is a sequel to *Approaching the Bible.*

The 7 Ws advocated in *Approaching the Bible* are applied to 40 difficult to understand passages. There are, of course, far more than 40 Problem Passages in the Bible. However, in this book Michael Penny not only solves these *40 Problem Passages*, but in doing so he equips the reader with a method by which many, many more hard to understand and difficult passages can be understood and successfully applied to the life of the believer today.

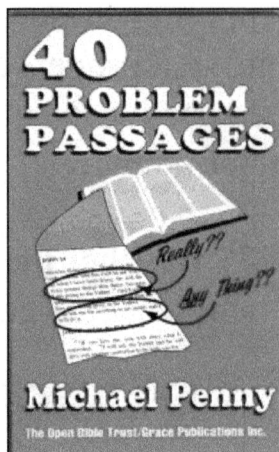

****

This book, and the ones on the previous pages, are also available as eBooks from Amazon and Apple,

and also as KDP paperbacks from Amazon.

About this book

Jacob

Abraham's great faith earned him the title, "The father of all who believed".

Isaac learned the lesson that "the fear of man brings a snare, but whoso puts his trust in Jehovah shall be safe."

Joseph stands out in a class by himself, a perfect type of Christ in his humiliation and exaltation.

But what have we to learn from Jacob? He was a man of low morals, continually scheming and plotting for his own benefit. But the author sees two outstanding lessons that all believers can learn from the life of Jacob:

- that grace overcomes the will of the flesh, and
- that faith overcomes the fear of man.

Publications of The Open Bible Trust must be in accordance with its evangelical, fundamental and dispensational basis. However, beyond this minimum, writers are free to express whatever beliefs they may have as their own understanding, provided that the aim in so doing is to further the object of The Open Bible Trust. A copy of the doctrinal basis is available at

www.obt.org.uk/doctrinal-basis

or from:

THE OPEN BIBLE TRUST
Fordland Mount, Upper Basildon,
Reading, RG8 8LU, UK.

www.ingramcontent.com/pod-product-compliance
Lightning Source LLC
Chambersburg PA
CBHW060616030426
42337CB00018B/3080